What People are Saying About *Just Me*

"Enough of the psycho-babble about parenting! This simple concise book is the instruction manual that should come with every child. It can eliminate years of therapy by showing you how to listen and understand your child from day one. *Just Me* is a compelling little read written from a child's silent perspective. And it shouts out 'JUST READ ME'!"

Paula R. Randall, mom/stepmom of five, freelance writer/producer

"Jackie is a genius! If parents would heed just half of these forty-three axioms, I (and Dr. Phil) would have much less to do as a clinical psychologist! These are not *some* of the answers to preventive mental health care, these are *all* the answers! Bravo!"

Robert N. Weinberger, Ph.D., Cofounder, National Parents' Network

"Where was this book when I was raising my children? This is the new map for navigating the complex minefield of parenting today."

Carolyn Weaver, mother of three and grandmother of five

"Jackie has so lovingly distilled the most basic truths essential for conscious parenting. Her compassion and sense of humor for the parent/child relationship is a breath of fresh air."

Alexandra Couvaras, Owner, Esperanza Schools

Just Me

What Your Child Wants
YOU To Know About Parenting

by just jackie

One Blue Button Publishing • Houston, Texas

Just Me
What Your Child Wants YOU To Know About Parenting
by just jackie

Published by:
One Blue Button Publishing
5090 Richmond, #182
Houston, TX 77056
www.onebluebutton.com

First Printing 2005

Copyright © 2005

ISBN 0-9762849-0-1

Printed in the United States of America by Malloy Printing, Ann Arbor, MI

Publisher's Cataloging-in-Publication
Jackie,Just.
        Just me: what your child wants YOU to know about
  parenting / by Just Jackie. -- 1st ed.
        p. cm.
        Includes index.
        LCCN 2004116124
        ISBN 0-9762849-0-1

        1. Parenting 2. Child rearing. 3. Parent and child.
        I. Title.

        HQ755.8.J33 2005   649'.1
                                     QBI04-800123

Cover Photograph: Ali, Age 7 by Gary Faye

About just jackie

Just jackie is typical of many multitasking moms in the twenty-first century. She is a wife, mother, mentor, entrepreneur, and marketing executive who nurtured her career and blended family simultaneously. When jackie married Bill Dryden, she had the awesome challenge of creating a family that embraced his two teen-age daughters as well as their new baby girl. Every day she wished she had the magic instruction manual that would pull everything together in a nice, neat, easy-to-read package, but it just didn't exist at the time.

Two decades later, all three girls have become thriving successful young women and jackie still wanted that simple concise book to give young friends who asked for her advice. So she decided to write it herself. Jotting down thoughts and feelings about being a parent and a child, her book began to take form. When faced with a serious brain surgery in 2004, she felt an even greater sense of urgency to finish the book but still needed the right creative angle. Within six months, her healing brain gave her the idea she craved, write the book from the child's point of view.

Today jackie lives in Houston with her husband, Bill, and continues to work in advertising while her role as a guest speaker on parenting continues to grow. Her work with national ad agencies has earned prestigious honors from the American Advertising Federation, Houston Advertising Federation, the New York Art Directors Club, as well as Commercial Art and PRINT magazines. She is a graduate of the University of Texas with a bachelor of journalism degree.

Dedication

This book is dedicated to the loving memory of my wonderful father, Morton L. Curtis. He taught me the beauty and importance of parenting each child as an individual, with love, compassion and patience. My favorite parenting advice he gave me was: never tell children not to put beans up their noses. They might not have thought about it until you mentioned it. Now you've given them something intriguing to try.

Thank you daddy for filling my heart and encouraging me to be boundless. I miss you every day.

Acknowledgements

My husband, Bill, for standing beside me for over two decades. You are my constant strength and my forever hero. I am amazed that I love you more each day. Me 'n You!

My daughter Ali. You are the light of my life and have made my job as a parent seem effortless. You are the most beautiful person I know - inside and out. I am inspired by your spirituality and blessed to share this journey with you. ILYSF!

My stepdaughters Cyndi and Stacy, for your love and support. You took me on as a stepmother during your challenging teen years and welcomed me into the family. I celebrate the exceptional women you have become.

My mother, Eleanor, for loving me unconditionally and teaching me the joys of motherhood. We have laughed and cried together and through it all stayed connected at the heart.

Special Thanks To:

My cousin, Pam Nelson for trusting in me and encouraging me to get this book out into the hands of parents everywhere.

Paula Randall for providing your wisdom and writing critique.

Dr. Jim Will and Fran for giving me wonderful direction and guidance in organizing my thoughts.

Kelli Kickerillo for supporting my passion and for believing in this book.

Janice Oaks and Richard McCarley for donating your valuable time and expertise.

You all played a very important part in making this book become a reality.

Dear Mom & Dad,

I know you don't have time to read a book on parenting – but there are some very important things I want to share with you. You may think you know most of this stuff. You may believe you already know everything you need to know to be a great parent. It can't be that hard, right? Well stick with me and read the following chapters in any order you want. Even read just one at a time. I guarantee you will find some guidance in building our relationship. I want you to really see me for who I am and realize that I am not like any other child. I am unique and our relationship should be based on you and me and nothing else.

"How to" parent is not in a book. It's in your heart and in my heart. This book is only a guide to help you learn to open up to me. It's written from my heart. I hope it will help you to see me for who I really am and who I can become with your love and support.

Let's learn to grow together in love, respect and kindness. I need you so very much and am depending on you to take me through my childhood and help me become a compassionate, wise, and moral adult. All the stuff that may seem simple can be the hardest to actually do. So please listen to me as I talk to you in this book and we can embrace each other in love and trust for many years. I'm so grateful that you bought this book and that you want to make our journey together the most amazing possible. I love you with all my heart!

Santiago   Age 5

I want to tell you about the most important things I need from you:

I Need Discipline and Structure

Please give me boundaries.
Make sure your rules are achievable.
Adjust the rules to fit my abilities and personality.

I Crave Love and Understanding

I am desperate for you to see me for who I am.
There is no other child just like me.
I can't survive without your touch and compassion.

I Want Guidance and Support

I look up to you.
Teach me about life and how to survive in the world.
I need to know you are on my side.

TABLE OF CONTENTS

I NEED DISCIPLINE AND STRUCTURE

I CRAVE LOVE AND UNDERSTANDING

I WANT GUIDANCE AND SUPPORT

I Need Discipline and Structure

Chapter 1

Be The Boss

You are the boss and I like it that way. No matter how much I may protest, I want to know that you are in charge. Remember I am a child and I do not have your life experience. I am counting on you to make the hard decisions for me. We should not have a tug-of-war with each other. I may not like what you say or do, but I want you to teach me the rules of our home. And I need you to insist that I follow them. You must set limits. Be clear about where the line is and let me know. I need structure. I crave guidance.

Don't let my temper tantrums or begging sway you to change your mind. When you tell me something, I want you to be firm. This makes me feel secure. And if you establish the guidelines when I am young and enforce them, I will stop pushing to change your mind.

But you don't need to be mean or harsh. I am growing and will make mistakes. Help me learn without feeling ashamed or bad about myself.

Being firm also means being fair. Explain things to me when we are calm in a way I can understand. Tell me up front what you expect and show me how to follow your rules. I want to make you happy, so please make your expectations realistic and appropriate for my age and capabilities. I may have to grow into some rules.

Set realistic boundaries, show me where they are and explain the consequences for stepping over the line. I can handle this.

Chapter 2

Say Less

When it comes to rules, focus on a few important ones – not hundreds of insignificant ones. If I am smothered in rules, I cannot ever get them all right. I will mess up. You are setting me up for failure. The more rules in our household, the more I am bound to break. Forgetting to pick up a sock should not be as important as chasing a ball into the street. If you punish or correct me for every broken small rule, I will give up trying to follow any of your rules and feel like I'll never get all the rules right. I will become angry and frustrated.

On the other hand, if you create lots of rules and never enforce any of them or are inconsistent in your punishment, you are teaching me to ignore all the rules. I'll consider them all unimportant and believe that breaking rules has no consequences. How can I distinguish between insignificant and important rules?

Make a few rules. Make them important ones. Make them clear. Make them achievable. And enforce them consistently. Keep your explanations brief.

Zoe   Age 5

Chapter 3

Be Truthful

Don't lie to me and expect me to be truthful. I will follow your lead on this subject and I am smarter than you think. I take everything in and remember what you say. Show me why telling the truth is important and help me to see the consequences of lying. I need to understand how my actions affect others and want you to guide me in developing strong character and integrity.

Teach me by example. Do not lie and then be alarmed if I do the same.

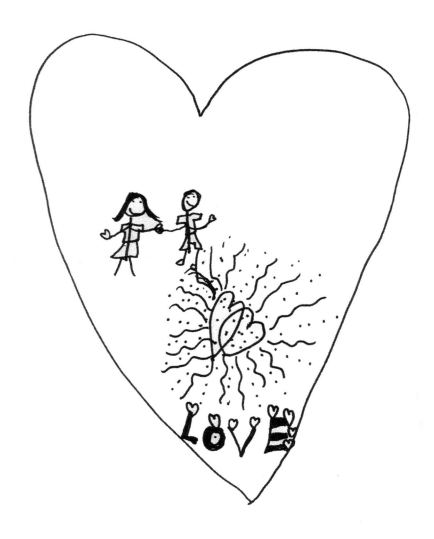

Alex   Age 8

Chapter 4

Be Consistent

No means no. I can handle this. Just be consistent. I don't need to get my way all the time. Even though I may pitch a fit, I will calm down quickly if I know that your "no" is firm and unwavering. It's when you change your mind that I get confused. If you say "no" and I cry and then you change to "yes," I learn to cry to get my way. The longer you let me cry the more persistent I will be, because I know you will eventually cave in. When you change your mind, you are encouraging me to whine and beg. And you know how unpleasant that can be.

I will manipulate you if you let me. But I should not be running the house, you should. Take control and let me know what is acceptable and what is not. I need firm rules that are consistently enforced to feel secure. If you are wishy-washy I will push you and test your patience - often!

Giving in to my whining may seem like an easy, quick fix, but it hurts us both in the long run. Stick to your decisions and mean "no" when you say it. I promise I can handle it.

Also, if Mom says no but Dad says yes, I will learn to use this to my advantage. I will turn each situation into a massive three-way struggle. If you guys get together and support each other in your decisions, it will be easier for me to accept your rules. United - you stand. Divided - I will conquer.

Chapter 5

Set Routines

I love routine. I need to know what to expect each day. I like to wake up at the same time and go to bed at the same time. You will get a lot less resistance from me if you are consistent with my schedule. I need lots of sleep and I need it to be a dependable part of my daily routine. Even if I say I am not tired, put me to bed at the same time each night and let me wind myself down. I may whine and complain, but if you are consistent, I will learn to enjoy and embrace rest. I crave bedtime rituals. Baths, stories, kisses and reassuring hugs are all great ways to get me ready to close my eyes. And I don't care if it's the same story every night. I just like this quiet time with you at the end of each day.

If you let me stay up late, I will be cranky the next day. If you let me change my bedtime on weekends there will be consequences. And they probably won't be pretty. It doesn't have to be a fight every night. Start when I am young and stick with a consistent bedtime. Even when I am in high school, I will need your guidance and persistence to help me get enough rest. I am happier, smarter and healthier when I get enough sleep. You need your rest, too.

You are giving me a wonderful gift when you teach me to spend some time alone learning to quiet myself. When I awake in the middle of the night please first make sure I am OK. But don't stay up with me or put me in your bed. That may seem like an easy solution at the time, but I will expect you to do this every time I am restless. When you let me quiet myself and get myself to sleep, I feel more contented and know you will be there if I really need you.

I also like my days to be predictable. If I go to a different place each day I feel unsettled and confused. How would you like to go to a different job each day and have to acclimate to new people and surroundings. Wouldn't that be much more stressful than going to a familiar place? In fact, when I am in school I will enjoy sitting at the same desk each day. I will feel more in control.

This doesn't mean that all my life needs to be predictable for me to be happy. I like new experiences and special fun days. Just let them be the exception and not the rule. I crave the security of routine.

Chapter 6

Be Specific

Be clear and concise. When you are either praising or correcting me, be specific. If you tell me, "You are such a good child," what does that mean? How do I earn that compliment again? Try saying, "Look how nicely you picked up your toys and put them on the shelf." Now I know you are pleased with me and why. I like hearing what you like about my behavior. I'm more likely to do it again. It may take more time and effort for you to be specific but it is so much more helpful to me.

And the same is true when you need to correct me. Although I may resist you, I do need your direction, critique and boundaries. If you say, "You are stupid," that's a damaging and hurtful thing to say. Don't criticize me for who I am, comment on what I did. Maybe I did something stupid, but I am not stupid. Try saying, "Don't ever run out in the street like that. You must always stop and look both ways to make sure no cars are coming before you get your ball." Let me know what I did wrong and how to change my behavior. Make sure you are clear, concise and specific. Good girl, bad girl comments are lazy parenting and they do not produce results.

LOVE

Amelia   Age 8

Chapter 7

Embrace God

Life is miraculous. And I am so glad we are on this amazing journey together. Please help me to open my life in praise to God for our many blessings. And guide me in sharing this grace with others.

Whether our family goes to a synagogue, church, mosque or simply worships in our own way at home, I want to acknowledge God's divine presence in my life. I need to praise my maker through the traditions, principles and customs that our family uses to worship. These rituals will help me through the difficult times in my life and provide the strength and wisdom I need to reach out to others.

I want to celebrate my connection with all human beings and I need to reconnect with my maker on a regular basis.

Allison   Age 9

Chapter 8

Teach Respect

Teach me to be kind to others. Let me know that every human being deserves respect.

If you laugh at people and talk behind others' backs, I will learn to do the same. I will believe it is OK to act this way. I will think it is acceptable to make fun of those who do not think or act like me. I may even fear or look down on those I don't understand. Show me how to have tolerance for others. Help me acknowledge beliefs and religions that are different from mine.

We are all human and feel the same pain, both physical and emotional. I don't want to become a person who believes it's OK to make fun of others and cause hurt. I want to be a healer and a kind human being. Model this behavior for me and I will keep my childlike love of everyone. I am born without prejudice. Only you and society can teach me to hate.

When I learn to respect others, I am free to be me.

Amy   Age 7

Chapter 9

Be Positive

I can follow a positive statement so much easier than a negative one. Tell me what you do want and stop telling me what not to do. Say, "walk slowly," instead of "stop running." Try, "Look how carefully you are carrying that glass," instead of, "Watch out... you're going to spill that."

Suggest a positive alternative to my negative behavior. This helps me learn how to change the behavior. I need this kind of direction. If you focus on what I am doing right, I will do more of that. If I can get your attention when I am behaving well and you let me know how you feel about the behavior, I will repeat the behavior. If I only get your attention by doing something wrong, I'll continue. I want your time and attention. I don't care what I need to do to get it. Try to notice me being good and tell me that you approve. "Look at you putting your toys away without even being asked. You must be so proud of yourself. I know I'm proud of you." Tell me what you do want and let me know how much you like it when I get it right.

Stop rewarding my bad behavior by giving in to me when I whine, beg or act up. If you pick me up and hold me every time I fuss, I will learn this is an effective way to get you to hold me whenever I want.

Your reactions guide my actions. This is a powerful concept.

Chapter 10

Whisper

Stop yelling. Say the important things softly. Train me to listen to you and not to block you out. Turn down the volume and I will learn to listen. When you constantly yell at me, I learn to yell back. I will assume that being loud is the best way to get someone's attention and make my point.

Try speaking quietly to me when you want to say something important. You will teach me to listen and to pay close attention. If I have to work to hear you, I will have to stop what I am doing and listen. If you yell all the time, I will also yell and not listen to what you say. It's too painful and it makes me feel bad to be constantly yelled at.

The loudest sound in our home should be laughter, not yelling.

Family Home

Aziza   Age 7

Chapter 11

Check Your Attitude

You know how easy it is for me to catch a cold? Just put me next to someone who is wheezing and sneezing and I'll be stuffy in no time. Well, attitudes are even more infectious than colds. I am a sponge. I absorb everything I see and hear. I am taking it all in. Do you want me to catch your attitudes about life? I am watching how you treat people and listening how you talk to and about others. You are my model for how to act as I grow up.

Do you always blame someone else for your problems or do you accept responsibility for your actions? Do you make fun of people who are not like you? Do you lie when it is convenient for you and cheat when you think you won't get caught? How can you expect me to learn respect when you are constantly grumbling about how other people act?

If you want me to love life, then let me see you embrace yours with joy and purpose. Remember that I am watching and listening. Teach me tolerance, respect and kindness. Attitudes are very infectious. Do you want me to catch yours?

Sydney   Age 6

Chapter 12

Tackle The Tough Stuff

Don't wait to talk about the tough stuff. Don't assume there will be a perfect time to discuss difficult topics. We need to continually confront the challenges of life every day. And sometimes this means opening up about bullies, cheating, friends, curfews, dating, alcohol, smoking, sex and drugs long before you think I am ready to tackle these subjects.

Although all conversations should be appropriate for my age, don't forget there are kids selling drugs at elementary schools. If you don't want me to learn about this stuff on the streets or through my friends or on TV, you need to tell me how you feel and what you think. I am watching you and listening to you. You are setting the example for my ethical code. If you cuss, smoke and engage in reckless behavior, chances are I will too.

Help me think through situations before I get confronted with them. Teach me alternate behaviors to help me deal with potential challenges. Role play with me and lead open discussions about how I might feel if I cave in to peer pressure. What will I think the next day? What might I say to avoid the situation altogether or to stand firm in my beliefs? When challenged, how can

I keep my self-esteem intact? What can I say when someone asks to cheat off my paper? How might I react when I see a bully pushing another kid on the playground? What can I do if I am coaxed into being intimate before I am ready? By role playing and acting out situations before they occur, I will be ready when something actually happens. I will know what my options and answers will be ahead of time. I will be less likely to be frightened, flustered or cave in to a difficult situation.

I will know what I want to do and why - before it happens. Because I will have already thought through the consequences of my actions and will have decided what is the right response for me. I will be ready for the tough challenges life is going to throw my way. I am growing up faster than you know and I need these discussions with you much sooner than you think. Don't be embarrassed. I will thank you for it later.

Chapter 13

Be Brief

Edit yourself. Suppress the urge to give me lengthy and involved explanations. Short, direct instructions are almost always better. When you go on and on I will tune you out and won't hear what you are saying. I will just hear, "You'd better not blah blah blah blah or I'll blah blah blah." Didn't you have a teacher who droned on and made you want to put your head on the desk and sleep? Long-winded instructions and explanations get ignored.

If you want to get my attention, be direct. If you want me to follow your directions, be brief. If I ignore you, be persistent. Don't say, "You'd better clean up your room. It's such a mess all the time. I don't know how you can find anything in there. I'm embarrassed to have company over for fear of what they will think. Why can't you pick up after yourself? Your room is a disaster." Try saying, " I expect you to pick up everything off your floor before dinner." You have a much better chance of connecting with me and getting the desired result.

As I grow I may need more elaborate explanations, but I will still most likely tune out a lengthy lecture. Get to the point. Be direct and be brief.

Brooke   Age 7

Chapter 14

Offer Choices

Help me learn to make good choices. If you decide everything for me, I will become too dependent. When I am ready, offer me choices and help me learn to take responsibility for my choices. Let me experience the consequences of my choices. Start with small, harmless choices and over the years you can help me learn to be independent and think for myself. This is a skill that will serve me well when the choices and the consequences become more serious.

When I am two, I can choose between yellow or white socks. When I am six, you can ask me if we should read a book together or tell stories. At twelve, I can decide between which should be first, math homework or piano practice.

Help me discover what it means to make decisions. I need to learn how to follow through with something I have started and then experience the consequences of my decisions - both positive and negative. When you give me little bits of control over my life, I will resist less when you need to step in and make important decisions for me.

And when I am old enough, have open discussions with me about some of the more challenging choices I will face. What options do I have, what are the possible consequences of my actions? When someone asks me if I want to smoke, I should be prepared with an answer. You and I should have already talked through this situation. You will have guided me to consider the possible responses and the consequences of each response. I should already know what my answer will be, and why. And it should be MY answer. I want to be a responsible decision-maker for my own life. But I need you to guide me through this process.

I Crave
Love
and
Understanding

Chapter 15

Listen Up

If you would spend more time listening to me and less time telling me what to do, I would be much happier. I came into this world with intelligence and purpose. I know what I need to feel good about myself and the world around me. If you just listen, I will guide you and help you learn how to parent me.

I didn't come with instructions for good reason. There are no absolutes or "right" answers to fit every child's needs. We do not all learn to walk at one. We are not all ready to read at five or six. We are not all afraid of the dark. Some of us don't want to be sports stars.

Listen to me. Watch me. Let me guide you and teach you what I need. You are usually so busy giving me instructions that you don't really hear what I am trying to say. Can you stop teaching and instructing long enough to focus on what I am saying?

If you want to make a true connection with me, listen to me. Teach me to vocalize my thoughts and feelings and really listen to what I say. Do you know what makes me happy, content, frightened, lonely, sad or restless? Help me open up so I can feel safe expressing myself to you. Listening is a skill I will be able to use in all my relationships.

Please don't tell me how I should feel. Listen to what I'm saying with my words and body language. Give me a safe place to share my hopes, feelings and fears. When I come to you with a problem, resist the temptation to try to immediately solve it for me. Ask me questions and assist me in working through possible outcomes. Help me talk my way through the situation without judging. Become my ally and source of comfort. You can guide me and help me discover solutions without forcing me to see it your way. I need to learn to think through a problem and discover the joy in conquering it myself.

The more you are able to listen without judging me, the more I will feel like sharing with you.

Chapter 16

Watch Your Words

Did you know that your words really can hurt me? It feels so awful when you yell and say ugly things to me. I wish you would take a few breaths and calm down before you try to tell me something. It's not that I don't want to hear you, I just can't understand you when you yell. I try to shut out the pain.

I will remember everything you tell me, and your harsh words will stay with me throughout my life. Think about why you are upset before you start to speak. Are you mad at me, at life, or with yourself? Are you angry at something I did or didn't do? You can correct my behavior without making me feel bad about myself. Tell me that you love me, but that you don't approve of what I just did. It helps me to get some positive reassurance before you let me know why you are displeased.

When you correct me, choose your words wisely. Don't say something to me that you wouldn't like someone to say to you. The wrong words can crush my spirit. Think before you speak.

Caroline   Age 6

Chapter 17

Lose The Labels

Do you remember being called the "smart one," "athletic one," "lazy one," or "quiet one"? How did that make you feel – superior, invisible, dumb? Did you like carrying that label? Or did you believe you were so much more than the label implied?

Why do parents put their children into compartments? Children are not like products in a pantry – boxes on the left and canned goods on the right. Does it make you feel more secure and in control? Does if give you a snappy answer when someone asks you about me? If I am the "smart one," how will I feel if I bring home a bad grade? Will you love me less?

I don't want to be categorized. When you label me you deny my complexity. You are not seeing me as a whole person. I am so much more than any label. See my multiple strengths and weaknesses and resist the temptation to define me by what I like to do.

I need you to encourage my talents and passions. Encouragement is good. However, the label can limit me from exploring and excelling in other things. I may be afraid to try something new if it doesn't fit my "label."

Sometimes I wonder if you love me for me or my accomplishments. I spend a lot of time trying to be what I think you want me to be. I may resist letting go of my label if I think I will lose your admiration, affection or attention. Who you believe me to be rubs off on me. See me for who I am, not for what I do. I am not a label, I am limitless!

Chapter 18

Validate Feelings

You seem so afraid of negative feelings. Why don't you want me to be mad, frustrated, or sad? Must I always be happy? Sure it's more pleasant to be around a happy person, but we all experience many different emotions throughout our lives. Why are some pushed away or hidden?

Let me know that it is normal to feel negative emotions. Let me see that sad, happy and angry are all valid feelings. All are a part of being human. Sometimes I just need a good cry to let off steam or to release my feelings. Crying is not always a bad thing.

Your challenge is to help me find safe and socially appropriate ways to express my feelings. Help me learn that there are some times and places that are better suited for dealing with my frustrations. Help me find a safe place to validate and express my negative feelings.

If I have a temper tantrum and throw myself on the floor kicking and screaming, it's a sure sign that I am overwhelmed or upset. Rather than commanding me to stop, simply send me to a quiet time-out spot. Tell me to go ahead and yell and scream and get it all out. This lets me know that it is OK to lose control but I need to do it without hurting anyone and without an audience. When I quit crying I can come back to you and get a hug.

Sometimes I will be sad and just need you to hold me and let me cry it out. Other times I need to learn to work it out by myself. Be a safe haven when I am hurting, disappointed, frustrated or angry. Help me learn how, when and where to express my many emotions.

Chapter 19

Be Wrong

Show me it is all right to be wrong. Let me know that being wrong does not mean I am stupid. How could anybody ever know everything and always be right? Trying to pretend you know it all is just plain silly. Why would you do that? Someone who thinks they are always right cannot be taught anything new. Being wrong is one of the greatest ways to learn and grow as a person.

Help me delight in looking for answers and information. Teach me the joy of learning rather than the habit of trying to always be right. I want to enjoy the process of learning. Set an example by showing me it's smart to admit you don't know something or might be wrong.

Some people can argue for hours over crazy little things. Does it really matter? Is it so hard to say, "You may be right"? This is not an admission of stupidity. It's simply an admission that you do not know everything. And you shouldn't cling to the illusion that you could.

Teach me that being wrong does not make me an inferior person. It makes me a growing, learning person. It gives me the courage to try and fail and try again without feeling dumb.   Show me that being wrong will happen a lot in my life. And the right way to be wrong is to use it as a chance to learn.

Chapter 20

Be My Cheerleader

Remember watching me learn how to walk? I walked all around the furniture holding on for what seemed like forever. You tried to get me to let go and walk on my own, but I just wasn't ready yet. Then one magical day, while holding onto the couch, I fixed my eyes on the chair that was three feet away. You knew by the look on my face that I was going to go for it. You held your breath and watched – trying not to distract me. Then it happened. I took two pitiful wobbly steps toward the chair and fell down halfway there. You probably didn't pick me up and say, "Now wasn't that pitiful! The chair is only three feet away and you couldn't even make it there without falling down. I'm so disappointed in you. You only made it halfway there and 50% in our society is failure. So I'm labeling you a failure at walking."

And you most likely didn't overload me with instructions such as, "Honey, just put your feet a little further apart and put your hands out for balance, like this." Both of those reactions would be mean and crazy. I'm sure you did what most parents do in this situation. You ran over to me, swooped me up and cheered me on. You called the family, neighbors and friends. You grabbed a camera and then put me back at the same spot on the couch where I started. You knelt by the chair I had been going for, reached your arms out to me and said, "Come on baby, try again! You can do it. I'm here to catch you if you fall." What a beautiful moment. You were my cheerleader. Encouraging. Safe. Loving. You made me want to try again, and again. You made me feel like I could do anything.

Why did you stop doing that? When did you decide that it was better to scold failure and dish out instructions for everything? I still need you to look at me with admiration and say, "Come on, I know you can do it. I'm here for you." Don't assume that as I get older that I don't need this anymore. I need you to nurture and cheerlead me through my failures. Trust me, encourage me and applaud my efforts. This is the path to my success. This is what I long for.

Encourage me more and scold me less when I fail.

Chapter 21

Just Relax

Chill out. Relax and let it go. How many times a day do you correct me? How often do you say "no," or "stop that"? Do you think you are molding me into a perfect human being by constantly correcting my behavior?

You know the various stages of my development are the pathways to my physical and emotional growth. I will mature at my own pace and in my own way. This doesn't mean that I don't need prodding, I just wish you would guide more than you correct. We need to work through things together and it's hard to feel you are on my side when I am constantly criticized.

Try not to pick at every little thing I do wrong, according to your definition of perfection. Let some of the small stuff slide and save your attention and direction for the important things. Striving to make me "perfect" will wear you out and place an unbearable burden on both of us. We will both end up stressed and frustrated.

Choose your battles wisely and learn to let life's little inconveniences, accidents and mistakes slide on by. We will have more harmony in our home and will build a stronger bond with each other if you are not picking at every little thing I do.

Relax your expectations and I will become more than you ever expected.

Chapter 22

Celebrate Differences

No two children are alike. So why would you try to parent us the same way? Many parents say, " I raised all my children in exactly the same way but they turned out to be so different." Well guess what... we are different. I come to you with my own set of needs and gifts. I want you to nurture me and help me discover my talents and my purpose in life.

Remember to delight in my uniqueness. Be flexible in your parenting to reflect my needs. I will thrive when you help me discover my strengths and adjust your parenting to fit me.

My rules may need to be slightly modified from my siblings. I will show you by my actions and words what I need. I hope you are paying attention. You have to see me based on my abilities, not on what you expect or know someone else might be capable of.

Aren't you glad that I am not like any other child?

Cassidy   Age 6

Chapter 23

Respect Learning

Are you a straight-A adult? Do you do everything well? Then why do you expect me to bring home nothing less than an A on my report card?

I was born with a natural curiosity. I actually love to learn. New accomplishments make me feel good about myself.

Schoolwork can be exciting when I am allowed to experience the joy of learning. But when I get graded in school, it seems like the focus is on what I don't know, not on what I have learned. This can make me sad and sometimes want to give up. So I will either push myself to get good grades – just for the grades, or I will shut down completely and stop trying or caring. The system that grades everything I do in school is very frustrating for me. I should love to learn and acquire knowledge. But grading me on each assignment teaches me to not be concerned with what I know, but only to focus on how to play the grade game. I might seek good grades to please you and my teachers and forget about learning.

Some kids can make straight A's without even trying. Some kids will never be able to make an A no matter how hard they try. Are they less valuable as people? Are they automatically less smart? As long as society judges my intelligence and worth by the grades I make, I may struggle to succeed and feel good about myself.

I will need your attention and support as I make my academic journey. Believe in me. Help me embrace the joy and excitement in learning. Don't zap my enthusiasm by obsessing over grades. I know I will need good grades if I want to go to college, but many successful people did not excel academically. I want you to help me learn how to study. But most of all, I want you to be realistic when you focus on my academic performance.

Chapter 24

Encourage Participation

What is the deal with winning? Is first place the only place good enough? Can I only be proud or feel good about myself if I win? Too much emphasis is placed on being a winner and not enough on being a participant.

The reason I should participate in competitive events is not to learn how to win. It should be to learn to work with others, build my physical abilities and sharpen my mental skills. I should also learn how to deal with success and failure as well as learn how to respect others while honoring my commitments. It should be about the excitement of being active and the joy of participation – not about outcome and winning.

Sure it's great to win, but if it is the only reason for doing something, we all lose. Trying to only be a winner is a huge burden for me. No one wins 100 percent of the time. Don't make me feel ashamed if I lose. Help me capture the excitement of participating in an activity and find the joy in just doing it.

Don't ask me if I won or lost. Ask me if I had a good time.

my brother
my sister
my dad
My Mom

Emily   Age 8

Chapter 25

Nurture Self Love

I will do just about anything to get your love. And I need you to show me and tell me why you love me. I must know that I can fail at anything and you will still love me. Don't let me think I must earn your love by acting a particular way or achieving certain goals. I want your unconditional love. I deserve it.

I also need to learn to love myself. This is so important to my happiness. I need to know that I am perfect just the way God made me. Help me get in touch with who I am and learn to appreciate all my talents and abilities. Together we can find out what I love most about being me. Rather than telling me, "I am so proud of you," try saying, "Great job! How does that make you feel about yourself?" Let me get in touch with my feelings to understand how the world around me affects them. This helps me rebound from disappointment and be gracious in success.

When I love myself it is easier for me to give to others and to feel comfortable helping them. I will be less likely to need to seek external approval for everything I do. If I am happy and content with who I am, I will rise to great heights.

Love me with all your heart. Let me know that nothing I do will cause me to lose your love. And teach me to look inwards at the magnificent person I am.

Chapter 26

Support My Dreams

I am not your second chance to live your dreams. I am not your "do over." I want you to let me be me. I may like some of the same things you do and I may look a lot like you did as a child, but I am not you.

Ask yourself if you are loving me for who I am or are you loving yourself through me? Try to see me for who I am, not for who you expect me to be. I am my own person. I have a lot to share with you and the world. I need your help to do this.

I know you have hopes and dreams for me, but they should center around wanting me to be healthy and happy. All the rest is insignificant. Whether I can throw a ball, play the piano or recite Shakespeare does not define my worth as a person. Let me chase my dreams, not yours. Understand I may change my mind often about what I want to do. I have to try something to know if I like it or not. Have patience with me during this process. Help me to persist and not give up too easily. With your support I will find my dreams.

Christopher   Age 8

Chapter 27

Promote Independence

You can help me most by teaching me to help myself. I want to learn to do new things every day. And I want to do them by myself when I can. When you trust me to do something on my own and I do it, I feel so proud of myself.

Start by letting go of the little things. Have tons of patience. Understand that I will not do them as quickly or as well as you, but this is what I need to learn, grow and gain control of my life and future. Wouldn't it be sad if you had to tie my shoes when I'm in high school because you never let me do it myself? I need you to challenge me with new tasks and responsibilities. Let me grow up step by step. Help me feel the pride in doing something by myself and for myself.

the Family tree

Daniel Age 8

Chapter 28

Keep Things In Perspective

Things will go wrong in our lives from time to time. Nobody can lead a perfect life. That would be so boring. How will you teach me to react when life deals me a blow? I will be watching how you react to disappointment and usually copy that behavior. If every little thing that goes wrong ruins your day, I will think that is the way it should be. If you yell and scream when things don't go your way, I will assume it is the right thing to do. I am always watching you because I want to be like you.

Consider this. When you are having an awful day and stuff is going terribly wrong, stop and ask yourself if any of it will matter in 200 years. Will it be family folklore? Will it be written about in history books? Will people still be discussing it? If the answer to any of these questions is yes, then you definitely have a right to be upset. If the answers are no, then do what you can to deal with it and let it go. Wouldn't it be better to show me constructive coping skills? I will benefit if I can watch you tackle a problem with a good attitude and show me how to move on. Bad things will happen in life. The only thing you have control over is how you handle them. Don't hold onto unimportant stuff and stew over it forever. Keep it in proper perspective.

Devina Age 7

I Want

Guidance
and
Support

Chapter 29

Hold On

The power of touch is amazing. More love can be communicated with a tender pat, a warm hug, or a soft kiss than with a hundred words. I need to feel safe and secure in your presence and soothed by your touch. Nurture me with long, loving embraces and I will grow up more relaxed and contented. There is nothing more magical than sitting quietly while being held in your arms. Our breathing and heartbeats connect in a magical way. Whether it is for a moment or an hour, take the time to share the gift of a loving touch with me on a regular basis.

Many times when I am fussy I can be calmed with a simple back rub or soft tickling of my arm. Or, I might need you to hold me tightly and rock me. When I know you are there I feel secure and loved.

If you only touch me when you are angry, I will avoid being close to you and learn to fear you. Touch me in kindness, not when you are upset. The need for your loving touch is something I will never outgrow.

Caroline   Age 4

Chapter 30

Be Still

Be silent. Be thankful. Take personal quiet time for yourself. It is so much easier to be a rational, caring parent when you are not totally frazzled.

At times life will be overwhelming. You desperately need a few minutes each day to stop, reflect and relax. I know the treadmill of parenthood seems to stay on high speed and can spin out of control. All the more reason you need to stop and at least catch your breath for a few moments. Learn to use your breath to calm and relax your mind and body. This is a wonderful gift to give yourself. And I will benefit from your clear head.

You may be able to only find five minutes alone a day or maybe only five breaths. Take it. Sit, close your eyes and breathe deeply and slowly. Fill your body with blood and oxygen, clear your brain and relax your muscles. You deserve this.

When I am old enough you can share this practice with me. Teach me to lie on the floor, close my eyes and just breathe slowly and deeply. I will love this quiet time with you. You will be showing me a skill I will be able to use throughout my life to rejuvenate and calm myself. Let's slow down.

Harrison   Age 8

Chapter 31

Imagine

One of my greatest gifts is my imagination. My ability to create is amazing. I have a wonderfully open mind that doesn't know what can't be done. I believe everything is possible. For me, fantasy and reality blend together.

Encourage my imagination. Help me use my mind to grow, discover, and learn about the magical side of life. Let's play, dream, draw, tell stories, sing and share. It's so rewarding to open my mind and connect with the infinite universe of possibilities.

I am a great inventor. Help me hang on to this gift. Let me know how much you admire my ability to create and I will continue to embrace my powerful sense of wonder and excitement. This does not mean I want to only live in a fantasy world. Real life will catch up with me soon enough. School, friends and eventually work will shower me with a heavy dose of reality. For now, help me exercise my imagination, stretch it and enjoy it to its fullest.

Ian   Age 5

Chapter 32

Be Joyful

Does my face light up when you enter the room? Do you bring me joy or fear? Are you "safe" to be around?

There are many frustrations in life, but why pass them on to me? Make our times together as joyful as possible. Show me how happiness is contagious and joy is a blessing. When I am happy with you, I will want to spend more time with you. Be a nurturing, safe person that I can come to with any questions or problems. If you are constantly cross or yelling at me, I will fear and resist you. Fear is not a good motivator. It may get temporary results but I will eventually withdraw from you and learn to hide my feelings. I won't want to be around you.

Now I don't expect you to be joyful all the time. There is a time for discipline and times when fatigue or other things will make you anger more easily. And there will be times when my behavior requires that you take stern action. But strive to bring as much joy as possible to our times together. Happiness is truly a choice we make. Show me how to embrace the good in life and celebrate each day with me. Find the joy in each day.

Jack   Age 5

Chapter 33

Let Go

Stop stressing over everything I do or don't do "on schedule." Sometimes you obsess over the craziest things. Your worries place unnecessary pressure on me. Don't bend out of shape if I am not ready to potty train when you think I should. I will get there when I am ready. Help me prepare and I'll let you know when it's time. I promise I won't go to high school in diapers!

There is no set age for anything. Some of us will cling to our "blankie" for years. Others might give up the bottle at one. Will I ever like vegetables? Why won't I let anyone hold me but Mom? Shouldn't I be walking by now? If I only eat cheese, will I be undernourished? Will the neighbors think you are a bad parent if............?

I will pass through many stages in my life. I may spend more time than others in a particular phase. This does not necessarily mean there is something wrong. If I can't tie my shoes just yet, relax. I will when I am ready. Your pushing me and stressing over every little thing will not help the process. It just makes both of us feel bad and creates tension between us.

As you let go, focus on the important things like love, attention, acceptance and listening. Observe me with love and delight in each stage of my development – no matter how long it seems to take.

Chapter 34

Book It

I love stories. They help my brain learn and grow. Please read to me often. I enjoy the pictures and I am soothed by the sound of your voice. Let's do this together every day, if possible. These are moments I will cherish forever. When we sit quietly together and become absorbed in a story, I am so content and connected.

When I am old enough, let me read to you. Have patience with me and let me take it at my own pace. Don't correct my mistakes too often or reading will lose its joy. This is more about togetherness and sharing than instruction. If I ask for your help give it to me. But please don't turn my reading for fun into a chore.

Reading is such a great way to learn about life and expand my creativity. It is a wonderful way to be exposed to different kinds of people, places and events. With your help I will learn to love reading for the rest of my life.

Please tell me stories, too. Make them up and make them fun. Teach me important life lessons this way. Tell me a story about sharing or learning to dress myself. Wrap life's lessons inside an interesting story and I will listen and learn. When I am old enough ask me to tell you a story. I find great delight in this. Plus it's a safe way to tell you about my day, my frustrations and accomplishments. Listen well. When I get stuck prompt me by saying things like, "What did the little boy do then?" Or, "Did she feel hurt when her friend was mean to her?" You will learn most of my stories are about what I know best - my life. Listen up and you will get to know me better and we will build an amazing connection during story time.

Chapter 35

Giggle

When was the last time you sang a silly song or did something really goofy? What happened to the fun-loving child in you? Please bring that child back out to play.

Did you lose your sense of humor? When did you decide to take all of life so seriously? I'd love for you to get down on the floor with me and giggle. Let's share the joy of letting go. Let's draw funny pictures and make up crazy stories. Remember how good it feels to loosen up and let go? I love these moments with you.

I need you to get on my level and be two, six, twelve or sixteen again. Just for a little while. Let's laugh till we cry and giggle till our faces hurt. You can learn a lot about how I am feeling about my life when you let go with me. I will open up to you and feel safe and happy. I'm not asking you to be my constant playmate, I simply want you to let loose and laugh with me from time to time. These are magic moments and treasured memories.

Jacob Age 9

Chapter 36

Be Here Now

Why do you think that the future will always be better and happier? Why does the past make you lose focus on today? There will always be joy and heartache. Each day comes with its blessings and challenges. So stop trying to get "there" and learn to connect with "here." You can never really get "there." You are always "here." Be here now. Be with me. Experience the peace of "now." Be fully alive in the present. If you constantly look to the future to solve your problems, or resent the past, you miss the opportunity to enjoy today - with me.

When a problem arises, ask yourself, "What can I do about it in the next fifteen minutes?" Tackle challenges in present tense. If you live life in fifteen-minute segments you only have to deal with present tense stress. Stop mulling over the past and having anxiety about the future. Live in the now. I want to experience today with you.

Many challenges lie in my future. Sometimes, it will be tempting to want to hurry through a difficult phase and get to the next stage in my development. When you do this, we both miss the joy of today and the big lessons we can learn from each stage of my development. Treasure each day with me. This day will never happen again.

Chapter 37

Write On

Sometimes it might be hard for you to express yourself to me. There are times when words don't work or just don't come easily. You may be too tired or frustrated or sad to be able to talk to me about your thoughts and feelings. At times like these, write your thoughts down. Put them in a book and save it for me. I can learn so much about you by reading this book some day. Or you can read it to me now if that will help us communicate and understand each other better. I want you to be able to express your feelings and be happy.

Some people are more verbal and others do better writing their feelings down. But, since I cannot tolerate constant verbal ranting, your writings will allow you to get things off your chest and relieve me of having to listen to a lengthy lecture. You still need to seize the moment and talk to me when something happens, just keep your comments direct and resist the need to tell me everything you are thinking. Make your point and then write the rest of it down in as much detail as you want. Save it for later. When you express your feelings in writing you help us both.

Jonathan   Age 7

Chapter 38

Draw Me Out

I do not have the vocabulary to accurately share my feelings. Sometimes I'm not even really sure what I am feeling, so it would be impossible to tell you. At times like these, when you see I need to express myself but feel too sad, angry or confused to speak, get out the crayons, markers and paper.

Sometimes I can draw, scribble and color my emotions much easier than I can voice them. Ask me to tell you how I am feeling on paper. It really feels good to get my feelings out in this way. You can learn a lot about what is going on in my life by looking at my drawings. What colors do I choose? What kind of images do I draw? What can I tell you about the drawings? If we do this exercise together often, you will get to know my moods by the kinds of pictures I draw. This will help us communicate in a non-verbal world where words are not needed.

Please don't comment too much about what I draw or critique my work. If you judge my drawings I will either start trying to draw to please you or stop doing them at all. The reason I am drawing is not to make pretty, framed pictures for you to put on the refrigerator.

Sometimes I will want to discuss what I have drawn and share it with you. Other times I won't want to talk about it at all. Either way, let my marks on the paper speak for me and let it be enough for now.

Chapter 39

Give Your Time

I know you want me to have stuff. You want to get the best stuff your income allows you to buy. You want me to have better stuff than you had growing up, which is great. I love toys, new clothes and playthings but stuff will never take the place of time with you.

When you sit me in front of the TV every day or leave me in my room alone for hours, I will adjust and try to find happiness with this kind of life. But you know how you enjoy a movie or ball game so much more when you share it with someone? Well, I'm just like that. Things do not really make me happy - experiences do. And I need you to help me engage my mind in interesting activities, not sit me in a room filled with stuff. Don't lead me to believe that one more doll or video game will make me content. That is a no-win situation.

Substitute stuff with time. I know you are busy and pulled in many directions every day, but I am growing up fast and soon you will be on your own again with more time to do all that "important" stuff. Show me that our time is much more meaningful than things.

Don't get fooled into believing that my participating in lots of activities is a good way to spend time with me. Sports, music, dancing and such can be great fun, if we are not stressed out by trying to do too much. And please make sure it is something I want to do, not something you are pushing me to do. That's worse than giving me too much stuff.

Just remember, I might enjoy the box more than the present itself. Time with you is always more valuable to me than stuff.

Chapter 40

Promote Health

Please don't feed me French fries and sodas. What are you thinking? There is no nutrition in these foods – only grease, salt and sugar. Is that any way to help me grow up healthy and strong? The first few years of my life are when I am growing most rapidly, both physically and mentally. How can you expect me to thrive when all you give me are processed, colored and preserved fast foods and sweets. What I really crave is real food; fresh fruits, vegetables and whole grains. These are the foods that make me feel good and healthy. Train me to listen to my body and let me eat when I am hungry and drink when I am thirsty. Don't force me to eat at a particular time or feed me too much. I will get enough nourishment if you offer me good food choices and take the time to prepare fresh, live food.

Give me raisins as a snack, not cookies. If we don't have junk foods in the house, I can't eat them. Never use food as a reward. Food is for nourishing the body, not for bribing me to do something. If you make me see food as a bonus for good behavior, I will use food to recapture the emotions associated with your approval. Food can become my friend or my foe. Help me acquire a taste for the earth's bounty.

I will be finicky and I will go through phases when I refuse to eat or will only eat one thing - for months. Relax, it's OK. This is perfectly normal. Don't force me to eat something just because you like it. I have my own tastes and I need to explore different foods to learn what I like. Just be sure to offer me good choices when I am hungry. Consider how you are training my taste buds and forming habits that will serve me my whole life.

Chapter 41

Get Active

Active people usually live longer, healthier lives. Isn't that what you want for me? Start me off with good physical activities early in life and I will see exercise as my friend, not as a chore. Movement fills the cells of the body with fresh blood and oxygen. When I exercise I am more alive, more alert and will sleep better. Exercise recharges my mind and body.

Just like good nutrition, exercise has benefits that can last a lifetime. Encourage my physical activity. Find things I enjoy and help me commit to a routine. Understand I may like something for a while and then change my mind. That's OK. I have to try different things to find out what I like. Help me see exercise as a natural part of my life. Let me discover the joy in participating in sports or dance or something that allows me to bend, stretch and build endurance.

Help me learn to exercise my physical self to get in touch with my body.

Sarah Age 7

Chapter 42

Recognize My Gifts

Before you criticize my behavior, consider this – I may simply be exploring my limits and discovering my talents. How high can I climb? How loud can I scream? How much water does the sink hold? I have to learn about life by living it. I know you want to keep me from repeating your mistakes but I will understand and retain more when I actually experience something. Now, I'm not asking you to let me engage in reckless behavior or hurt myself. But let me have room to explore my talents and gifts. Sometimes it just feels good to bang spoons together or sing a song over and over and over. I will learn what is acceptable behavior at home and what may be inappropriate in public. I will sometimes test your patience, but remember I am only exploring life.

If I run everywhere, I may be telling you that I love running. If I talk too much, I may grow up to be a teacher or speaker. If I love to paint pictures, I may be a budding artist or designer. Be careful what you criticize me for – it may turn out to be my greatest gift. If you see my actions as growth and not just my being unruly, you can help me learn to refine and channel my behavior and discover my unique talents. Don't squash my spirit. Splashing in the puddles sometimes just feels good – remember?

Larson Age 5

Chapter 43

Look Ahead

Thanks for taking the time to read this book. Has it helped you understand me a little better? There is so much more I want to say but this is a great start. I'm sure you can think of many things I might have forgotten. Share them with me when you can. It would be fun to hear what you have to say about the ideas in this book.

We've only just begun and I am excited about our future together. We are connected at the heart forever.

This would be a good time for you to put down this book, give me a hug, look me in the eyes and start really connecting.

Mary Elizabeth   Age 8

Index

The Artists of The Post Oak School

A special thanks to the students of The Post Oak Montessori School in Houston, Texas for the amazing artwork displayed throughout this book. The school nurtures the joy of learning in each student and produces happy, competent and considerate young boys and girls. It is a privilege to share their drawings on the subjects of love and family.

Alex	Age 8	Page 22	Emily	Age 8	Page 66
Amelia	Age 8	Page 28	Harrison	Age 8	Page 80
Allison	Age 9	Page 30	Ian	Age 5	Page 82
Amy	Age 7	Page 32	Jack	Age 5	Page 84
Aziza	Age 7	Page 36	Jacob	Age 9	Page 90
Brooke	Age 7	Page 42	Jonathan	Age 7	Page 94
Caroline	Age 4	Page 78	Larson	Age 5	Page 104
Caroline	Age 6	Page 50	Mary Elizabeth	Age 8	Page 106
Cassidy	Age 6	Page 62	Rachel	Age 8	Page 109
Christopher	Age 8	Page 70	Santiago	Age 4	Page 10
Daniel	Age 8	Page 72	Sarah	Age 7	Page 102
Devina	Age 7	Page 74	Sydney	Age 6	Page 38
Elizabeth	Age 6	Page 110	Zoe	Age 5	Page 20

Rachel   Age 8

Elizabeth   Age 6